THE WONDER
BIBLE
STORYBOOK

THE WONDER BIBLE STORYBOOK

Text by Pauline Youd
Illustrated by Elaine Garvin

Copyright © 2003 Scandinavia Publishing House
Drejervej 15,3 • DK–2400 Copenhagen NV • Denmark
Tel (+45) 3531 0330 • E-mail: jvo@scanpublishing.dk
Web: www.scanpublishing.dk

Design by Ben Alex
Text copyright @ Pauline Youd
Illustrations copyright @ Elaine Garvin
Printed in Singapore

ISBN 87 7247 280 4

THE WONDER
BIBLE
STORYBOOK

Text by Pauline Youd
Illustrations by Elaine Garvin

scandinavia

CONTENTS

WHY DID
SARAH LAUGH?

*T*hen the LORD said, "I will surely return to you about this time next year, and Sarah your wife will have a son."

Now Sarah was listening at the entrance to the tent, which was behind him. Abraham and Sarah were already old and well advanced in years, and Sarah was past the age of childbearing. So Sarah laughed to herself as she thought, "After I am worn out and my master is old, will I now have this pleasure?"

Then the LORD said to Abraham, "Why did Sarah laugh and say, 'Will I really have a child, now that I am old?' Is anything too hard for the LORD? I will return to you at the appointed time next year and Sarah will have a son."

Sarah was afraid, so she lied and said, "I did not laugh."

But he said, "Yes, you did laugh."

Now the LORD was gracious to Sarah as he had said, and the Lord did for Sarah what he had promised. Sarah

became pregnant and bore a son to Abraham in his old age, at the very time God had promised him. Abraham gave the name Isaac to the son Sarah bore him. When his son Isaac was eight days old, Abraham circumcised him, as God commanded him. Abraham was a hundred years old when his son Isaac was born to him.

Sarah said, "God has brought me laughter, and everyone who hears about this will laugh with me." And she added, "Who would have said to Abraham that Sarah would nurse children? Yet I have borne him a son in his old age."

Genesis 17: 10-15; 21: 1-7, NIV

WHY DID SARAH LAUGH?

Sarah was 89 years old. Her husband, Abraham, was 99 years old. They wanted a baby.

But they were too old to be parents. They prayed to God for a baby. But God said, "Wait."

One day some visitors came. Sarah made dinner while
Abraham talked to the visitors.

   Sarah wanted to hear what they said, so she hid behind
the tent curtain and listened.

"Sarah will have a baby," one of the visitors said.

Sarah laughed. She knew she was too old to have a baby.

"Why did Sarah laugh?" asked the visitor. "Is anything too hard for the Lord?"

8

Abraham came to the tent. He saw
Sarah making dinner.

"I didn't laugh," Sarah lied.

Abraham went back to the visitors.

9

"Yes, she did laugh," the visitor said. "But this time next year she will have a baby."

The next year, when Sarah was 90 years old, and Abraham was 100 years old, God said "Yes" to their prayer. Sarah had a baby boy.

Sarah was so happy. And God told Abraham to name the baby Isaac, which means "laughter."

God didn't think Sarah and Abraham were too old to be parents.

Did you ever think something was too hard for God to do? That's what Sarah thought in the story. God wants us to know that he listens to all our prayers. God wants us to know that he answers all our prayers.

But sometimes God says "Wait" when we ask for something. That does not mean God doesn't love us. It does not mean that God can't do what we've asked him to do. It just means that God has something better he wants to give us or do for us. God knows what is best for us! God always does what is best for us!

13

14

"Sarah said, 'God has brought me laughter, and everyone who hears about this will laugh with me.' And she added, 'Who would have said to Abraham that Sarah would nurse children? Yet I have borne him a son in his old age.'"

Genesis 21:6-7

WHY WAS
PHARAOH PUZZLED?

**The story about Pharaoh and Joseph
is taken from Genesis, chapter 41.**

*S*o Pharaoh sent for Joseph, and he was quickly brought from the dungeon. When he had shaved and changed his clothes, he came before Pharaoh.

Pharaoh said to Joseph, "I had a dream, and no-one can interpret it. But I have heard it said of you that when you hear a dream you can interpret it."

"I cannot do it," Joseph replied to Pharaoh, "but God will give Pharaoh the answer he desires."

"It is just as I said to Pharaoh: God has shown Pharaoh what he is about to do. Seven years of great abundance are coming throughout the land of Egypt, but seven years of famine will follow them. Then all the abundance in Egypt will be forgotten, and the famine will ravage the land. The abundance in the land will not be remembered, because the famine that follows it will be so severe. The reason the dream was given to Pharaoh in two forms is that the matter has been firmly decided by God, and God will do it soon."

The plan seemed good to Pharaoh and to all his officials. So Pharaoh asked them, "Can we find anyone like this man, one in whom is the spirit of God?"

Then Pharaoh said to Joseph, "Since God has made all this known to you, there is no-one so discerning and wise as you. You shall be in charge of my palace, and all my people are to submit to your orders. Only with respect to the throne will I be greater than you."

Genesis 41:14-16; 28-32; 37-40, NIV

WHY WAS
PHARAOH PUZZLED?

Pharaoh had a very
strange dream.
It woke him up.
  The dream puzzled him.
What did it mean?
  Pharaoh didn't know, so he
went back to sleep.

22

But Pharaoh dreamed another strange
dream that woke him up.

Pharaoh was very puzzled.

He called his wise men and told them
his dreams.

"What do my dreams
mean?" he asked.

The wise men didn't know.
"There is a man named
Joseph who knows what
dreams mean," one
wise man said.
Pharaoh called
Joseph in and told
him his dreams.

24

"I dreamed about seven fat cows and seven skinny cows," Pharaoh said. "But the seven skinny cows ate up the seven fat cows. Then I went back to sleep and dreamed another dream.

"I dreamed about seven fat ears of corn and seven skinny ears of corn.

"But the seven skinny ears of corn ate up the seven fat ears of corn. I am puzzled. Can you tell me what my dreams mean?"

"God helps me know
what dreams mean," said
Joseph. "The two dreams mean
the same thing. The seven fat cows
and the seven fat ears of corn mean seven
years with plenty of food.

"The seven skinny cows and the seven skinny
ears of corn mean seven years when there will be
no food. You need someone to collect food during
the seven good years. Then you will have food to
give the people during the seven bad years."

"I will do what you say," said Pharaoh. "Your
God has made you very wise."

Now Pharaoh could sleep well. He wasn't
puzzled any more.

27

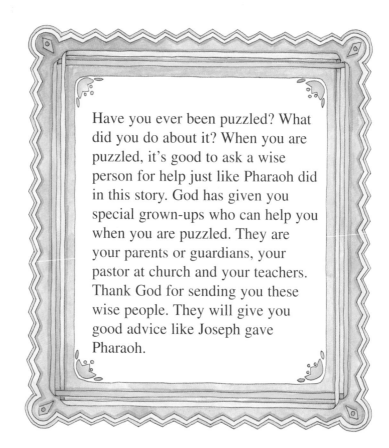

Have you ever been puzzled? What did you do about it? When you are puzzled, it's good to ask a wise person for help just like Pharaoh did in this story. God has given you special grown-ups who can help you when you are puzzled. They are your parents or guardians, your pastor at church and your teachers. Thank God for sending you these wise people. They will give you good advice like Joseph gave Pharaoh.

"Since God has made all this known to you, there is no-one so discerning and wise as you. You shall be in charge of my palace, and all my people are to submit to your orders. Only with respect to the throne will I be greater than you."

Genesis 41:39

WHY WAS
DEBORAH MAD?

The story about Deborah is taken from The Book of Judges, chapter 4.

*A*fter Ehud died, the Israelites once again did evil in the eyes of the LORD. So the LORD sold them into the hands of Jabin, a king of Canaan, who reigned in Hazor. The commander of his army was Sisera, who lived in Harosheth Haggoyim. Because he had nine hundred iron chariots and had cruelly oppressed the Israelites for twenty years, they cried to the LORD for help.

Deborah, a prophetess, the wife of Lappidoth, was leading Israel at that time. She held court under the Palm of Deborah between Ramah and Bethel in the hill country of Ephraim, and the Israelites came to her to have their disputes decided. She sent for Barak son of Abinoam from Kedesh in Naphtali and said to him, "The LORD, the God of Israel, commands you: 'Go, take with you ten thousand men of Naphtali and Zebulun and lead the way to Mount Tabor. I will lure Sisera, the commander of Jabin's army, with his chariots and his troops to the Kishon River and give him into your hands.' "

Barak said to her, "If you go with me, I will go; but if you don't go with me, I won't go."

Then Deborah said to Barak, "Go! This is the day the LORD has given Sisera into your hands. Has not the LORD gone ahead of you?" So Barak went down Mount Tabor, followed by ten thousand men. At Barak's advance, the LORD routed Sisera and all his chariots and army by the sword, and Sisera abandoned his chariot and fled on foot. But Barak pursued the chariots and army as far as Harosheth Haggoyim. All the troops of Sisera fell by the sword; not a man was left.

Judges 4: 1-8; 14-16, NIV

WHY WAS DEBORAH MAD?

People always came to Deborah for advice.
She had good answers to their problems.
  "My wisdom comes from God," Deborah said.
"God loves me and protects me."
  When the people came to Deborah,
she told them, "God loves you,
too, and will
protect you."

One day some people came and told
Deborah they were being attacked. Their
enemies took their land. Their enemies
took their animals. Their enemies took
their weapons so they couldn't fight back.

Their enemies took their land and their animals. They even made them slaves. That made Deborah mad! She shook her finger at the people.

"Don't let them do that!" she said. "Where are your strong men who will stand up for you?"

The people hung their heads. "We only know one man
who has courage," they said.

"Go get him," commanded Deborah.

The people brought Barak.

"Go and fight the enemy!"
said Deborah. "God loves you
and will protect you."

"I'm afraid to go alone," said
Barak, "but I will go if you will
go with me."

That made Deborah *very* mad.

She shook her finger at Barak. "I will go,"
she said, "but a woman will get credit for
winning the war. You will not!"

Barak called the army and fought against the
enemy.

Deborah prayed to God and God helped
Barak win the war.

Barak knew God loved him and gave him
courage.

That made Deborah happy.

Did you ever know someone bigger and stronger than you who wanted to start a fight with you? What did you do?

If you pray, God can help you at times like that. He can give you wisdom like he gave Deborah. He can show you ways to make peace with those who start trouble. He can give you courage like he gave Barak. God will always show you the right thing to do if you ask him!

45

"Go! This is the day the LORD has given Sisera into your hands. Has not the LORD gone ahead of you?"

Judges 4:14

WHY WAS GIDEON WORRIED?

*T*he angel of the LORD came and sat down under the oak in Ophrah that belonged to Joash the Abiezrite, where his son Gideon was threshing wheat in a winepress to keep it from the Midianites. When the angel of the LORD appeared to Gideon, he said, "The Lord is with you, mighty warrior."

"But sir," Gideon replied, "if the LORD is with us, why has all this happened to us? Where are all his wonders that our fathers told us about when they said, 'Did not the LORD bring us up out of Egypt?' But now the LORD has abandoned us and put us into the hand of Midian."

The LORD turned to him and said, "Go in the strength you have and save Israel out of Midian's hand. Am I not sending you?"

"But Lord," Gideon asked, "how can I save Israel? My clan is the weakest in Manasseh, and I am the least in my family."

The LORD answered, "I will be with you, and you will strike down all the Midianites together."

Gideon and the hundred men with him reached the edge of the

camp at the beginning of the middle watch, just after they had changed the guard. They blew their trumpets and broke the jars that were in their hands. The three companies blew the trumpets and smashed the jars. Grasping the torches in their left hands and holding in their right hands the trumpets they were to blow, they shouted, "A sword for the Lord and for Gideon!" While each man held his position around the camp, all the Midianites ran, crying out as they fled.

> *When the three hundred trumpets sounded, the LORD caused the men throughout the camp to turn on each other with their swords. The army fled to Beth Shittah towards Zererah as far as the border of Abel Meholah near Tabbath.*

Judges 6:11-16; 7:19-22, NIV

WHY WAS
GIDEON WORRIED?

Gideon was a soldier. He fought against God's enemies. He trusted God, but sometimes he worried.

54

One day some people called the Midianites
came with a big army to fight against Gideon.
God wanted Gideon to trust him so he said,
"Your army is too big, Gideon. The people
will think their own strength has won the war.
Tell the soldiers who are afraid, to go home."

Gideon asked his soldiers, "Who is afraid to fight the Midianites?"

Twenty-two thousand soldiers said they were afraid! So Gideon told them to go home.

Gideon was worried. He only had 10,000 soldiers left to fight the Midianites.

But God said, "Your army is still too big. I will divide the soldiers again."

Gideon took his soldiers to the creek to get a drink. Three hundred soldiers cupped the water with their hands and drank. The rest of the soldiers got down on their hands and knees and put their mouths in the water.

God said, "Keep only those soldiers who cupped the water with their hands."

Gideon was worried. But he did what God told him to do.

Then God said, "Now your army is just the right size."

Gideon said, "If we win with only 300 soldiers, the people will know that God helped us."

Gideon and his soldiers fought the Midianites. Gideon's army won. Now Gideon wasn't worried. He had learned to trust God more. And all the people knew that God had helped Gideon win the battle.

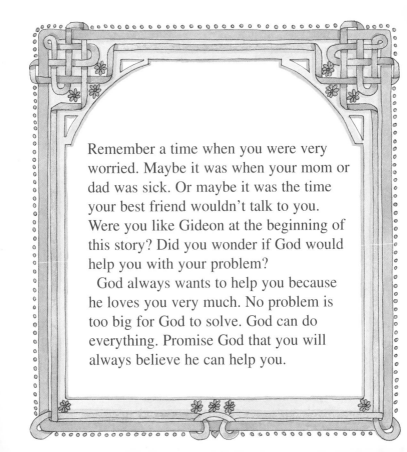

Remember a time when you were very worried. Maybe it was when your mom or dad was sick. Or maybe it was the time your best friend wouldn't talk to you. Were you like Gideon at the beginning of this story? Did you wonder if God would help you with your problem?

God always wants to help you because he loves you very much. No problem is too big for God to solve. God can do everything. Promise God that you will always believe he can help you.

61

*"When the angel
of the LORD appeared
to Gideon, he said, 'The
Lord is with you,
mighty warrior.'"*

Judges 6:12

WHY WAS
DAVID BRAVE?

*T*hen (David) took his staff in his hand, chose five smooth stones from the stream, put them in the pouch of his shepherd's bag and, with his sling in his hand, approached the Philistine.

Meanwhile, the Philistine, with his shield-bearer in front of him, kept coming closer to David. He looked David over and saw that he was only a boy, ruddy and handsome, and he despised him. He said to David, "Am I a

dog, that you come at me with sticks?" And the Philistine cursed David by his gods. "Come here," he said, "and I'll give your flesh to the birds of the air and the beasts of the field!"

David said to the Philistine, "You come against me with sword and spear and javelin, but I come against you in the name of the Lord Almighty, the God of the armies of Israel, whom you have defied. This day the LORD will hand you over to me, and I'll strike you down and cut off your head. Today I will give the carcasses of the Philistine army to the birds of the air and the beasts of the earth, and the whole world will know that there is a God in Israel. All those gathered here will know that it is not by sword or spear that the LORD saves; for the battle is the LORD's, and he will give all of you into our hands."

As the Philistine moved closer to attack him, David ran quickly towards the battle line to meet him. Reaching into his bag and taking out a stone, he slung it and struck the Philistine on the forehead. The stone sank into his forehead, and he fell face down on the ground.

So David triumphed over the Philistine with a sling and a stone; without a sword in his hand he struck down the Philistine and killed him.

I Samuel 17: 40-50, NIV

WHY WAS DAVID BRAVE?

"Come out and fight me
What's the matter?
Are you afraid?"
Goliath's laughter
rumbled across the vall

The Israelite army shook with fear, for Goliath was nine feet tall and wore heavy armor. He also carried a huge spear on his shoulder.

Every day Goliath shouted at the Israelites, "If I win, you will be our servants. But if you win, we will be your servants."

David's brothers were soldiers in the Israelite army. When David came to visit them, he saw Goliath and heard him shout.

"Who is this giant who dares the army of the
living God?" David demanded. "I will go out
and fight him myself."

"You are only a boy," the soldiers said.

But David answered, "God will protect me.
When I kept my father's sheep and a lion or
bear took a lamb out of the flock, I went after it.

"I rescued the lamb and killed both the lion and the bear.

"This giant will be just like one of them, for he has made fun of the living God's army."

David took five smooth stones and ran with his sling toward the giant.

Goliath's laughter rumbled across the valley when he saw the little shepherd boy coming.

But David shouted, "You come to me with a sword and a spear, but I come to you in the name of the Lord!"

He put a stone in the sling and twirled it around and around. Then he let it go.

The stone struck Goliath between the eyes and he fell face down on the ground.

The Israelite soldiers cheered.

Because of David's faith in God, he was braver than all the soldiers.

75

Do you know anyone who
makes fun of people who love God?
That's what Goliath did in the story.
Do you know anyone who uses the name of
God in a disrespectful way? God made the
world and all that is in it. He deserves our
praise. God gave us life. He deserves our
worship. God is a living God who loves us.
He deserves our love. Promise God you
will always praise him, worship him, love
him and thank him.

"You come against me with swordand spear and javelin, but I come against you in the name of the Lord Almighty."

I Samuel 17:45

WHY DID
ELIJAH HIDE?

The story about Elijah is taken from I Kings, chapters 18-19

*E*lijah was afraid and ran for his life. When he came to Beersheba in Judah, he left his servant there, while he himself went a day's journey into the desert. He came to a broom tree, sat down under it and prayed that he might die. "I have had enough, LORD," he said. "Take my life; I am no better than my ancestors." Then he lay down under the tree and fell asleep.

And the word of the LORD came to him: "What are you doing here, Elijah?"

He replied, "I have been very zealous for the LORD God Almighty. The Israelites have rejected your covenant, broken down your altars, and put your prophets to death with the sword. I am the only one left, and now they are trying to kill me too."

The LORD said, "Go out and stand on the mountain in the presence of the LORD, for the LORD is about to pass by."

Then a great and powerful wind tore the mountains apart and shattered the rocks before the LORD, but the LORD was not in the wind. After the wind there was an earthquake, but the LORD was not in the earthquake. After the earthquake came a fire, but the LORD was not in the fire. And after the fire came a gentle whisper. When Elijah heard it, he pulled his cloak over his face and went out and stood at the mouth of the cave.

Then a voice said to him, "What are you doing here, Elijah?"

I Kings 19:3-5; 9-13, NIV

WHY DID ELIJAH HIDE?

Elijah ran and ran. He was
looking for a place to hide.
Wicked Queen Jezebel wanted
to kill him.

Elijah found a cave where
Queen Jezebel couldn't find him. He was
very tired and hungry. He felt very sad and discouraged.
Elijah thought God didn't love him any more.

86

But Elijah was God's prophet and God did love him. God told him to get up and stand at the door of the cave.

Elijah saw a great wind storm, but he didn't see God.

Next Elijah felt a great earthquake, but he didn't see God.

Then Elijah saw a great fire, but he still didn't see God.

Finally, Elijah heard the quiet voice of God. Elijah listened very carefully.

God said, "Elijah, why are you hiding in a cave?"

Elijah cried, "Queen Jezebel is going to kill me!"

Then Elijah moaned and complained to God, "I have been your prophet, but you don't seem to care about me. I'm the only one left who believes in you."

89

God answered, "You are not the only one left.
There are 7,000 others that you don't know about.
But I have a very important job just for you,
Elijah, and Queen Jezebel will not be able to stop
you. Come now."

Elijah believed God and did what God said.
Elijah didn't have to hide any more

91

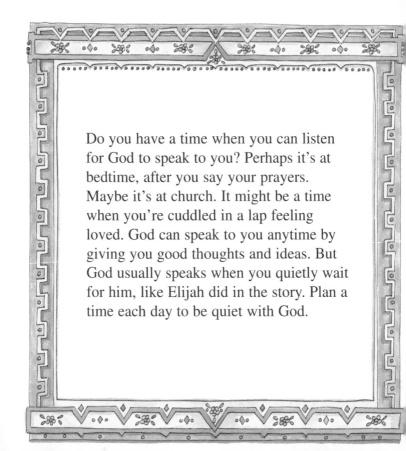

Do you have a time when you can listen for God to speak to you? Perhaps it's at bedtime, after you say your prayers. Maybe it's at church. It might be a time when you're cuddled in a lap feeling loved. God can speak to you anytime by giving you good thoughts and ideas. But God usually speaks when you quietly wait for him, like Elijah did in the story. Plan a time each day to be quiet with God.

*"What are
you doing here,
Elijah?"*

I Kings 19:9

WHY WAS
DANIEL SCARED?

So the king gave the order, and they brought Daniel and threw him into the lions' den. The king said to Daniel, "May your God, whom you serve continually, rescue you!"

A stone was brought and placed over the mouth of the den, and the king sealed it with his own signet ring and with the rings of his nobles, so that Daniel's situation might not be changed. Then the king returned to his palace and spent the night without eating and without any entertainment being brought to him. And he could not sleep.

At the first light of dawn, the king got up and hurried to the lions' den. When he came near the den, he called to Daniel in an anguished voice, "Daniel, servant of the living God, has your God, whom you serve continually, been able to rescue you from the lions?"

Daniel answered, "O king, live for ever! My God sent his angel, and he shut the mouths of the lions. They have not hurt me, because I was found innocent

in his sight. Nor have I ever done any wrong before you, O king."

The king was overjoyed and gave orders to lift Daniel out of the den. And when Daniel was lifted from the den, no wound was found on him, because he had trusted in his God.

At the king's command, the men who had falsely accused Daniel were brought in and thrown into the lions' den, along with their wives and children. And before they reached the floor of the den, the lions overpowered them and crushed all their bones.

Daniel 6: 16-24, NIV

WHY WAS
DANIEL SCARED?

Daniel lived in a land far from his home.
The people who lived there didn't worship God.
But Daniel loved God and prayed to him every
day. He knew God was always with him
even though his own family and friends
could not be. Daniel knew God heard
his prayers and would
help him.

The king of the land where
Daniel lived liked Daniel. Some
of the king's officials noticed this.
They grumbled, "The king likes
Daniel better than he likes us."
Others whispered, "Let's get
Daniel in trouble."

103

The officials knew Daniel prayed to God, so they decided to trick the king into writing a law that made praying to God a crime. The king signed the law, but Daniel still prayed to God.

The officials told on Daniel. They said he had to die because he disobeyed the new law. So the king had to put Daniel in the lions' den.

Was Daniel scared? The lions were big. They had strong jaws and sharp teeth. They were very hungry. Daniel looked like he would taste good.

What did Daniel do? He did what he always did when he was scared. He prayed and asked God to help him.

What did God do? He closed the lions' mouths so they couldn't hurt Daniel!

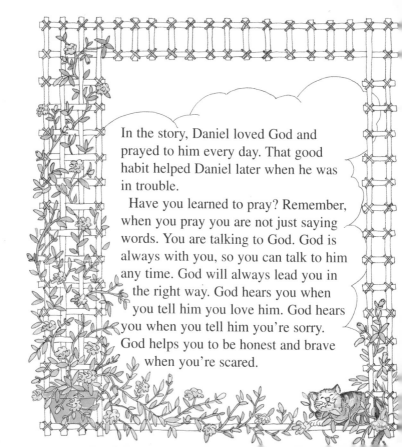

In the story, Daniel loved God and prayed to him every day. That good habit helped Daniel later when he was in trouble.

Have you learned to pray? Remember, when you pray you are not just saying words. You are talking to God. God is always with you, so you can talk to him any time. God will always lead you in the right way. God hears you when you tell him you love him. God hears you when you tell him you're sorry. God helps you to be honest and brave when you're scared.

109

"And when Daniel was lifted from the den, no wound was found on him, because he had trusted in his God."

Daniel 6:23

WHY WAS
JEREMIAH SAD?

The story about Jeremiah is taken from Jeremiah 1; 38:1-13;
II Chronicles 36:15-23; Nehemiah 2.

*T*hey were angry with Jeremiah and had him beaten and
imprisoned in the house of Jonathan the secretary,
which they had made into a prison.

*Then the officials said to the king, "This man should be put to
death. He is discouraging the soldiers who are left in this city,
as well as all the people, by the things he is saying to them.
This man is not seeking the good of these people but their
ruin."*

*"He is in your hands," King Zedekiah answered. "The
king can do nothing to oppose you."*

*So they took Jeremiah and put him into the cistern of
Malkijah, the king's son, which was in the courtyard of the
guard. They lowered Jeremiah by ropes into the cistern; it had
no water in it, only mud, and Jeremiah sank down into the mud.*

*But Ebed-Melech, a Cushite, an official in the royal
palace, heard that they had put Jeremiah into the cistern. While
the king was sitting in the Benjamin Gate, Ebed-Melech went
out of the palace and said to him, "My lord the king, these men
have acted wickedly in all they have done to Jeremiah the*

prophet. They have thrown him into a cistern, where he will starve to death when there is no longer any bread in the city."

Then the king commanded Ebed-Melech the Cushite, "Take thirty men from here with you and lift Jeremiah the prophet out of the cistern before he dies."

So Ebed-Melech took the men with him and went to a room under the treasury in the palace. He took some old rags and worn-out clothes from there and let them down with ropes to Jeremiah in the cistern. Ebed-Melech the Cushite said to Jeremiah, "Put these old rags and worn-out clothes under your arms to pad the ropes." Jeremiah did so, and they pulled him up with the ropes and lifted him out of the cistern. And Jeremiah remained in the courtyard of the guard.

Jeremiah 37:15; 38:4-13, NIV

WHY WAS JEREMIAH SAD?

Jeremiah loved to read God's word. He knew it was the truth. It said if people obeyed God they would be happy, but if they disobeyed God they would be punished.

118

The people around Jeremiah didn't read God's word.

They were unkind and selfish.

They wouldn't help the poor and needy.

"God doesn't see us," they said. That made Jeremiah sad.

119

God told Jeremiah to tell the people
they were disobeying his word.

The people made fun of Jeremiah.

God told Jeremiah to tell them they
would be punished.

But the people turned their backs
on Jeremiah.

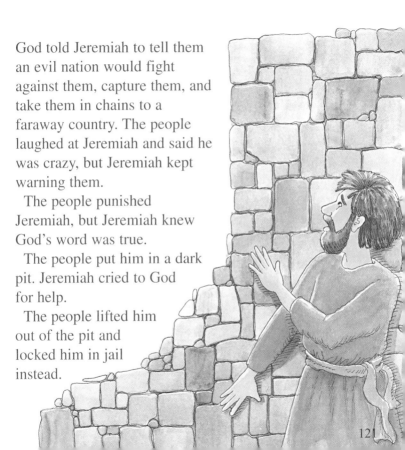

God told Jeremiah to tell them an evil nation would fight against them, capture them, and take them in chains to a faraway country. The people laughed at Jeremiah and said he was crazy, but Jeremiah kept warning them.

The people punished Jeremiah, but Jeremiah knew God's word was true.

The people put him in a dark pit. Jeremiah cried to God for help.

The people lifted him out of the pit and locked him in jail instead.

121

But Jeremiah didn't stop warning the people.

How he wished they would read God's word!

How he wished they would believe God!

How he wished they would be kind!

But the people would not obey God.

An evil nation did come and fight against them. They captured the people and led them away in chains.

Jeremiah cried and cried. He was sad because the people would not listen to God.

He was sad because they would not obey God.

Many years later the people told God they were sorry. They believed God's truth and returned to their land.

123

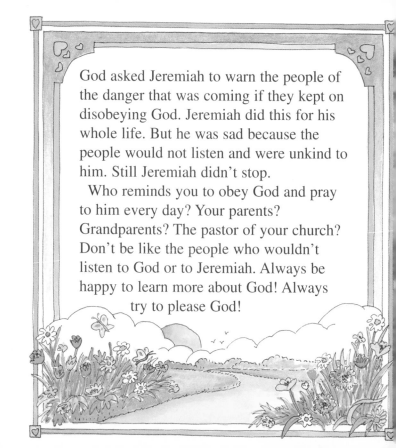

God asked Jeremiah to warn the people of the danger that was coming if they kept on disobeying God. Jeremiah did this for his whole life. But he was sad because the people would not listen and were unkind to him. Still Jeremiah didn't stop.

Who reminds you to obey God and pray to him every day? Your parents? Grandparents? The pastor of your church? Don't be like the people who wouldn't listen to God or to Jeremiah. Always be happy to learn more about God! Always try to please God!

"My lord the king, these men have acted wickedly in all they have done to Jeremiah the prophet. They have thrown him into a cistern, where he will starve to death when there is no longer any bread in the city."

Jeremiah 38:9

WHY DID NEHEMIAH WORK SO HARD?

The story about Nehemiah is taken from Nehemiah 1-6.

*T*hey said to me, *"Those who survived the exile and are back in the province are in great trouble and disgrace. The wall of Jerusalem is broken down, and its gates have been burned with fire."*

When I heard these things, I sat down and wept. For some days I mourned and fasted and prayed before the God of heaven.

Then I said to them, "You see the trouble we are in: Jerusalem lies in ruins, and its gates have been burned with fire. Come, let us rebuild the wall of Jerusalem. . . ."

But when Sanballat the Horonite, Tobiah the Ammonite official and Geshem the Arab heard about it, they mocked and ridiculed us. "What is this you are doing?" they asked. "Are you rebelling against the king?"

I answered them by saying, "The God of heaven will give us success. We his servants will start rebuilding, but as for you, you have no share in Jerusalem or any claim or historic right to it."

Therefore I stationed some of the people behind the lowest points of the wall at the exposed places, posting them by

families, with their swords, spears and bows. After I looked things over, I stood up and said to the nobles, the officials and the rest of the people, "Don't be afraid of them. Remember the Lord, who is great and awesome, and fight for your brothers, your sons and your daughters, your wives and your homes."

So the wall was completed on the twenty-fifth of Elul, in fifty-two days. When all our enemies heard about this, all the surrounding nations were afraid and lost their self-confidence, because they realised that this work had been done with the help of our God.

Nehemiah 1:3-4; 2:17-20; 4:13-14; 6:15-16, NIV

WHY DID NEHEMIAH WORK SO HARD?

Round and round Jerusalem Nehemiah rode. What did he see? Broken walls, burned gates, piles of broken stones everywhere.

Nehemiah cried. God's special city was in ruins. "We must rebuild the wall and make Jerusalem safe," he said.

134

"Yes," the people agreed. "We will rebuild the wall."

The people worked very hard.

Sanballat, Tobiah and Geshem were enemies of God. They didn't want the wall rebuilt. They laughed at Nehemiah and pointed their fingers.

"That wall is too weak," they said. "It won't hold up a little fox."

But Nehemiah and the people kept building.

Sanballat, Tobiah and Geshem lied about Nehemiah.

"You just want to make yourself king of Jerusalem," they said.

"That isn't true," said Nehemiah and he kept building.

Sanballat, Tobiah and Geshem planned to attack
the city.

But Nehemiah prayed to God.
He gave the people weapons to
protect themselves.

With their weapons in one
hand and ready to fight, they
kept rebuilding the wall.

Finally the wall was finished.
Only the gates needed to be built.

Sanballat, Tobiah
and Geshem said to
Nehemiah, "Can't
we talk this over?
Meet us outside the
city."

137

138

But Nehemiah said, "No, I'm far too busy to stop and meet with you."

Then a man came and said, "Hide in the temple, Nehemiah! Sanballat, Tobiah and Geshem are going to kill you."

"I will not hide in the temple," said Nehemiah. "God will protect me while I finish the gates."

Finally, round and round Jerusalem Nehemiah rode.

He saw tall, strong walls with gates.

Nehemiah and the people shouted for joy.

Jerusalem was safe.

Did you ever start out to do something important and then get side-tracked? You meant to keep on cleaning your room, but a friend came over. You meant to take out the garbage after lunch, but you forgot. You meant to do your homework, but you got sleepy.

In the story, Nehemiah kept on building the wall no matter what. That was what God wanted him to do. When he finished, he shouted for joy.

Learn to finish what you start. Then you'll feel happy. Just like Nehemiah!

141

"Don't be afraid of them. Remember the Lord, who is great and awesome, and fight for your brothers, your sons and your daughters, your wives and your homes."

Nehemiah 4:14

WHY WAS MARY EMBARRASSED?

The story about Mary
is taken from The Gospel of John, chapter 12.

Six days before the Passover, Jesus arrived at Bethany, where Lazarus lived, whom Jesus had raised from the dead. Here a dinner was given in Jesus' honour. Martha served, while Lazarus was among those reclining at the table with him. Then Mary took about a pint of pure nard, an expensive perfume; she poured it on Jesus' feet and wiped his feet with her hair. And the house was filled with the fragrance of the perfume.

     But one of his disciples, Judas Iscariot,

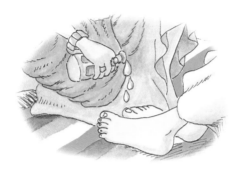

who was later to betray him, objected, "Why wasn't this perfume sold and the money given to the poor? It was worth a year's wages." He did not say this because he cared about the poor but because he was a thief; as keeper of the money bag, he used to help himself to what was put into it.

"Leave her alone," Jesus replied. "It was intended that she should save this perfume for the day of my burial. You will always have the poor among you, but you will not always have me."

John 12: 1-8, NIV

WHY WAS MARY EMBARRASSED?

Mary took a beautiful bottle down from the shelf. Holding it with both hands, she turned it around and around in the candlelight. She lifted the lid. The sweet smell of perfume filled the room.

Mary quickly put the cover back on the bottle. She looked across the hallway to the living room. Dinner was over. Jesus was sitting with his disciples around the low table talking to Mary's brother, Lazarus.

151

Jesus was a very special friend of their family. He had taught them about God's love.

Jesus had made Mary's brother, Lazarus, alive and well. Mary was very grateful to Jesus. She wanted to do something special for him.

Suddenly Mary had an idea.

She clutched the bottle and walked into the room where the men sat talking.

Kneeling beside Jesus, Mary lifted the lid and poured the perfume on Jesus' feet. Then she wiped his feet with her hair.

One of the men jumped up and cried, "What a waste! Why didn't you sell that perfume and give the money to the poor?"

Mary was very embarrassed. Her face turned red. She wanted to run out of the room.

Then she felt Jesus' gentle hand on her shoulder. "Leave her alone, Judas," Jesus said to the man. "She gave me this gift because she loves me. What she has done for me will be remembered and talked about for thousands of years."

155

Do you like to give gifts? Almost everyone does. Most of the time we try to give what we think the other person really wants. But how do you feel when someone laughs at your gift or acts like he or she doesn't want it? Mary gave Jesus the most precious thing she had. She gave it because she loved him. Jesus was happy to accept Mary's gift.

The most precious thing you can give Jesus is your love. Jesus said, "If you really love me, you will obey my teaching." Have you ever thought of your obedience as a gift to Jesus? It's a gift only you can give him.

Supplies

LITTLE LEAGUE

157

"Leave her alone," Jesus replied. *"It was intended that she should save this perfume for the day of my burial. You will always have the poor among you, but you will not always have me."*

John 12:7-8

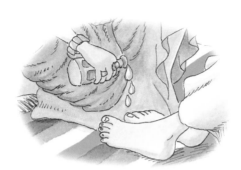

WHY WAS THE
SHEPHERD GLAD?

The story about the good shepherd is taken from The Gospel of Luke, chapter 15

*J*esus told them this parable: "*Suppose one of you has a hundred sheep and loses one of them. Does he not leave the ninety-nine in the open country and go after the lost sheep until he finds it? And when he finds it, he joyfully puts it on his shoulders and goes home. Then he calls his friends and neighbors together and says, 'Rejoice with me; I have found my lost sheep.' I tell you that in the same way there is more rejoicing in heaven over one sinner who repents than over ninety-nine righteous persons who do not need to repent.*"

Luke 15:3-7, NIV

WHY WAS THE
SHEPHERD GLAD?

The shepherd counted his sheep as they went through the opening into the sheepfold.
1 - 2 - 3 - 4. . . .
He counted and counted.
5 - 6 - 7 - 8. . . .
He counted till finally the last sheep was in.
98 - 99 - *Wait!*

50-51·

166

One sheep was missing! There should be 100 sheep in the sheepfold, but there were only 99!

The shepherd rolled a rock in front of the door of the sheepfold and started out. He must find his other sheep.

167

Over the first hill he went with his staff in his hand. Down through the valley he searched. He looked and looked. Up another hill he went. The sun was setting. Soon it would be dark.

The shepherd was very worried. Fierce animals roamed the hills at night. They would attack a sheep who was alone.

168

The shepherd started down into another valley. *Wait!* What was that tiny sound he heard? His little sheep was calling for help!

The shepherd saw some thick bushes. The bushes had sharp thorns. The sheep was caught in the bushes. He was struggling to get free. But the sharp thorns pulled at his wool and scratched his face.

170

The sheep's legs were dirty and covered with blood. "Baa-baa-baa," he cried.

The shepherd carefully pushed back the branches and gently lifted the sheep onto his shoulders.

He carried the sheep up the hill and down the valley, up the other hill and down to the sheepfold.

Once inside the sheepfold he washed the deep scratches and put medicine on them. He hugged the sheep. "Now all my 100 sheep are safe!" he exclaimed. "I'm so glad I found you!"

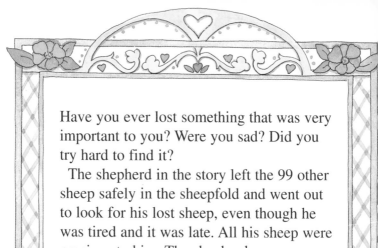

Have you ever lost something that was very important to you? Were you sad? Did you try hard to find it?

The shepherd in the story left the 99 other sheep safely in the sheepfold and went out to look for his lost sheep, even though he was tired and it was late. All his sheep were precious to him. The shepherd was very glad when he found his missing sheep.

Jesus is our Good Shepherd. He never leaves us. If one of us wanders away from him, he always brings us back. Jesus loves each one of us with a very special love!

173

"There is more rejoicing in heaven over one sinner who repents than over ninety-nine righteous persons who do not need to repent."

Luke 15:7

WHY WAS
ANDREW SURPRISED?

**The story about Andrew is taken from
The Gospel of John, chapter 6.**
(See also Matthew 14, Mark 6 and Luke 9)

When Jesus looked up and saw a great crowd coming towards him, he said to Philip, "Where shall we buy bread for these people to eat?" He asked this only to test him, for he already had in mind what he was going to do.

Philip answered him, "Eight months' wages would not buy enough bread for each one to have a bite!"

Another of his disciples, Andrew, Simon Peter's brother, spoke up, "Here is a boy with five small barley loaves and two small fish, but how far will they go among so many?"

Jesus said, "Make the people sit down." . . . .
Jesus then took the loaves, gave thanks, and distributed to those who were seated as much as

they wanted. He did the same with the fish.

When they had all had enough to eat, he said to his disciples, "Gather the pieces that are left over. Let nothing be wasted." So they gathered them and filled twelve baskets with the pieces of the five barley loaves left over by those who had eaten.

After the people saw the miraculous sign that Jesus did, they began to say, "Surely, this is the Prophet who is to come into the world."

John 6:5-14, NIV

WHY WAS
ANDREW SURPRISED?

"Where can we buy enough bread to feed all of these people?" Jesus asked his friend Philip.

The crowd of people had come to hear Jesus teach about God his father. They had listened all day, but now it was suppertime and Jesus knew they must be hungry.

182

"We can't afford to feed all these people," said Philip.

Andrew heard Philip and Jesus talking.

"There is a boy here who has five little loaves of bread and two small fish," Andrew told them, "but that's all."

"Bring the boy to me," Jesus said to Andrew.

183

So Andrew brought the boy with his five loaves and two fish to Jesus.

"May I use what you have to feed these hungry people?" Jesus asked him.

The boy smiled and gave his supper to Jesus.

"Tell the people to sit down on the grass," Jesus told his disciples. The people sat down and Jesus prayed. "Thank you, God, for giving us this food," he said.

Then Jesus took the loaves and the fish and gave them to his disciples to give to all the people.

185

The people ate and ate. Everyone had as much to eat as he or she wanted.

"Take baskets and collect all the leftovers so no food will be wasted," said Jesus.

The disciples collected twelve baskets full of leftovers.

"But we only had five loaves of bread and two small fish," Andrew whispered to Philip.

Andrew was very surprised because Jesus had fed more than 5,000 people with that bread and fish!

With only five small loaves and two fish, Jesus fed 5,000 people. Andrew was surprised that Jesus could use small, ordinary things to work a miracle.

What small things can you offer for Jesus to use? Can you play the piano or draw pictures? Can you be a peacemaker among your friends? Will you give Jesus part of your weekly allowance by putting it in the collection at church? Give Jesus a helpful attitude at home and watch him work a miracle!

189

"Here is a boy with five small barley loaves and two small fish, but how far will they go among so many?"

John 6:9